K'UNG FU TZE

A DRAMATIC POEM

BY

PAUL CARUS, 1852-1919.

己所不欲 勿施於人

"What ye wish not done unto you,
Do ye not unto others."
—*Confucius.*

LONDON   CHICAGO
THE OPEN COURT PUBLISHING CO.
1915

181.112
C277k

FOREWORD.

In the present work, "K'ung Fu Tze, a Dramatic Poem," the author does not intend to offer a drama of the usual style, with thrilling adventures, plots and hairbreadth escapes, but, as the subtitle states, "a dramatic poem." In a most concise form adapted to the stage, the composition represents Confucianism in its origin and according to the sources. Dramatic action and stage effects, which we would not be without in the drama, have not been overlooked; in fact they are obviously present. But the author's main object has been to work out for the English-speaking public a presentation of the Chinese religio-ethical world-conception in the dramatized life of its founder, K'ung Nî, commonly called K'ung Fu Tze, who has moulded the history of China and is still the main factor in the public and private life of his native country.

In undertaking a work of this kind, which in the author's opinion is a highly desirable task, the temptation at once offers itself to sacrifice truth to beauty, or rather to the taste of to-day; to neglect history for the sake of art, i.e., of ephemeral art interpretation; and to change the traditional figure of our hero into a modernized manikin who would be likely to arouse the applause of the galleries. It is a temptation, and the temptation is great because it promises success; it would be irresistible if the object were pecuniary profit. And it would be so easy! It is much easier to let a sage who lived almost two and a half millenniums ago speak like a reformer of to-day and to adapt the age in which he attempted to introduce his ideals, to the customs and thoughts of our own days. Moreover, we could invent thrilling and impossible stories of court intrigues, of our hero's rise to power and his final downfall, and the result would be that the audience would find entertainment for an evening, the spectators would applaud and go home satisfied. The author has abstained from modernizing the subject except where certain modernizations are indispensable to render it intelligently into a modern language. But the author has not written for glory, nor has he contemplated a business success on the stage. His intention is to chisel out in dramatically presentable form the character and destiny of a man who has been the hero in the moral development of a great nation. He has not ventured to change the main outlines of tradition, not because he was too pedantic to do so, but because he sees in the history of human development a higher mode of art. History to him appears as a divine drama, whose author is God himself.

In ancient Greece the drama was a religious performance and at Athens it was deemed so important that citizens were paid a day laborer's price to enable even the poor man to attend it. In this country the drama is a business proposition designed to while away the evening by a pleasing entertainment. The time may come when the artistic feature of the drama will be in demand. In many cities theaters are closed on Sundays; but the true drama is religious in its inmost nature and is or ought to be as good as, if not better than, a sermon in church.

Tradition is in the habit of idealizing its heroes, and that is part of history. It was not Jesus who founded the church, but Christ; not Gautama Siddhartha who gave rise to Buddhism, but the Tathagata, the World-honored Buddha; not Mohammed who established Islam, but the Prophet; and these factors existed before the persons in whom they became incarnate and who developed into superpersonalities after their deaths. This is the case also with Confucius. The ideal of a sage, a superior thinker, an overman, a master, existed before Confucius, and Confucius believed in the ideals of the past. He laid no claim to supernatural revelation, but later generations adopted his doctrines as inspired, as infallible, as divine.

Upon the whole the author has followed tradition, for he did not deem it right in this drama to make innovations or to substitute modern views for the old Chinese ideals. Confucius appears here as he is represented in Confucian literature, not always to our taste, not as a warlike Saxon, not as a bold reformer like Luther, not as a brave fighter or original thinker, or as a pioneer, but as a prophet of peace, as a quiet enthusiast for authority and an admirer of the venerable past that has laid the basis for civilization. The changes which have been introduced for the sake of adapting certain events to dramatic effectiveness are few and of secondary significance. So in history the man who married the niece of Confucius was not Mang-I himself but Nan Yung, probably a cousin of Mang-I. The name of the sage's niece is not known nor is her character an absolute type of the Confucian ideal of womanhood, but this deviation is made purposely. The ideal woman of Confucian ethics would be almost impossibly monotonous, and we know from the Book of Odes that some of the actions and sentiments of Chinese women were more human than the sage himself would approve.

The scene that is placed near the end of Act II did not happen in Lo after the meeting with Lao Tze in 518 B. C., but much later in Confucius's life, in 495, in Chang, south of the state of Wei. I will also mention that Confucius was called to office in 497, much later than might be assumed by the context of this drama; at least, the lapse of nineteen years between Acts III and IV is not emphasized. Likewise the incident of the crazy man referred to in the second scene of Act IV also happened about ten years earlier.

The picture here given is genuine in all essential points, and the contrast between Confucius and his rival, the philosopher Lao Tan (*alias* Lao Tze), is true to life. We see the man K'ung as he was, and Confucianists will have no reason to find fault with the characterization of their master.

The author has neither added embellishments to, nor detracted aught from, the man and his ideals; nor have the defects of the great teacher been hidden. Indeed we can understand how the habitual teaching and moralizing must sometimes have excited the admiration of his contemporaries and sometimes have bored them. Above all, we shall find

here an opportunity to understand the great success of the
sage by considering the impression he made on his contem-
poraries as well as on succeeding generations. We see before
us the *esprit de corps* that ensouled his disciples whose love
and faith finally elevated their master to the high plane of
a divine prophet, to the rank of such men as Zarathustra,
Buddha, Christ and Mohammed.

It is a question whether such subjects as the lives of these
great religious leaders should be dramatized at all, but the
author is strongly inclined to affirm that the deepest problems
of mankind, the religious solutions of the world-riddle as
offered under different conditions in past ages by the leaders
of human thought, are most appropriate subjects for dramatic
presentation, and the time will come when our theater-going
public will demand to see them. Then the poet should not
offer fantastic fabrications out of the wealth of his imagina-
tion, but should make himself the mouthpiece of that greatest
of all poets, God,—the God of history, the God of human
progress, the God of evolution.

In this spirit and with this ideal in view, the present
dramatic poem has been written, and, if this style of dramatic
treatment should not be according to the taste of the present
generation, the author feels that the future is preparing when
it will find response and be appreciated.

*   *   *

A few comments may be added to explain the Chinese
world-conception.

God, in the proper sense of the word, the one and only
God, creator and sustainer of the world, has been known in
Chinese history since time immemorial under the name of
SHANG Tî, the Lord on High. However, Shang Tî has
not been in immediate touch with the minds and consciences
of the Chinese people. His recognition is more theoretical
and does not enter into practical life. He is worshiped by
the emperor annually in a holocaust offered him at Peking
on the altar of Heaven.

Though Shang Tî is always spoken of as a personal God,
he is frequently identified by philosophers with a philosophic

principle.   Confucius speaks little of Shang Tî, but much of
Heaven in the sense of Providence, and Lao Tze calls God
wan wuh chi tsung, which means "Ancestor" or "Arch-
Father of the ten thousand things" (see the *Tao Teh King* or
The Canon of Reason and Virtue, Chap. IV, 1).   Lao
Tze practically lets aboriginal reason, the Tao, take the place
of Shang Tî in the sense of the divine principle that governs
the world, and these views are quite common throughout the
writings of Chinese philosophers.

According to the Chinese world-conception all things are
assumed to be mixtures of two opposites, the YANG and the
YIN, of which Yang is the positive, and Yin the negative ele-
ment.   The former means strong, lord-like, luminous, and is
represented in nature by heaven; the latter, being womanly,
weak, submissive, is represented by earth.   The former was
originally pictured as a white disk, thus: ○, and later on as a
straight whole line, thus: ——; the latter originally as a
black disk, thus: ●, later as a broken line, thus: — —.
In their combination they were represented by a peculiar
symbol, thus, ☯ called *T'ai Chi,* which means the Great
Ultimate or the Grand Extreme, also translated the Ulti-
mate or Absolute.*   *Chi* originally denoted the gable of a
roof, and so represents the idea of the topmost or ultimate
outcome of thought, or as western philosophers would say,
"the Absolute."   In its undifferentiated form it is com-
monly represented as a luminous orb.

A Chinese philosopher would make the same statement
that we find in the Bible, "In the beginning God created
the heaven and the earth;" but he would interpret the words
"heaven and earth" in a more general sense, in a philosophical
and almost mathematical conception, meaning by heaven the
principle Yang and by earth the principle Yin.

In Chinese history the founder of civilization was Fu Hi.
He was the first of the primitive five rulers of China, and he
was credited with the invention of writing, or rather of

---

*Also transcribed *T'ai Kih.*   See the author's *Chinese Philosophy,*
pp. 24 ff.

thought symbols, especially the combinations of the Yang and Yin in sets of three, called in Chinese *kwa* or trigrams.

Later on, the trigrams were doubled and formed hexagrams, sixty-four combinations of which are possible, and the mystical meaning of these constitutes the subject matter of the ancient Book of Changes, called in Chinese *Yih King*.

The Yih King[1] is a book of divination, and tradition connects with it the fate of Wen Wang, the ancestor of the imperial house of Chow. Details with regard to this man and his sons, Wu Wang and Chow Kung, are well worth knowing on account of the significance they possessed in the opinion of Confucius. Wen Wang, i. e., "Scholarly Ruler," is the posthumous appellation of Ch'ang whose title in his lifetime was Si Peh, i. e., "Chief of the West." He was hereditary chieftain of the principality of K'i in the territory of the modern Shen-si. The last emperor of the house of Yin, Chow Sin, characterized in Chinese history as "the abandoned tyrant," caused Ch'ang, the Chief of the West, to be imprisoned, because one of the imperial advisers, Hu, the earl of Ts'ung, regarded him as dangerous on account of his virtues.

While held in durance for two years at Yew Li, the "Scholarly Ruler" pondered over the meaning of the *Yih*, the changes or permutations of the hexagrams, and derived from them the hope of a final delivery and a brighter future. His expectations were fulfilled, and his son Fa, best known under the posthumous title Wu Wang, crossed the Hwang Ho at the ford of Meng and overthrew the abandoned tyrant Chow Sin in battle on the plains of Muh, whereupon he was recognized as emperor.

Wu Wang was supported by his younger brother, Tan, the fourth son of the Chief of the West, Wen Wang, and known in history as Chow Kung, the Duke of Chow. On the death of his imperial brother, Wu Wang, this Duke of Chow acted

1. On the *Yih King* see the author's *Chinese Philosophy*, p. 7, and *Chinese Thought*, pp. 26-36. As to the probable connection which this method of divination had historically with the Urim and Thummim, see *The Oracle of Yahveh*, pp. 27-34.

as guardian of his nephew, the child emperor, and his virtue
is praised as highly as that of the ancient rulers Yao and Shun.

*   *   *

Confucius was born in 551 B. C.   At 17 years of age he
held a position as superintendent of an estate.   The first
and second acts of our drama play in the year 518 B. C.,
when Mang-I, the son of the minister Mang Hsi, joins the
sage and they visit together the city of Lo, capital of the
state Chow, and the home of the old philosopher Lao Tze.
The second act takes place soon after the return of K'ung
Tze and Mang-I to their home in the state of Lû.   In the
third act we find Confucius installed as minister of justice,
but he feels compelled to leave his post on account of the
arrival of the singing damsels sent to Duke Ling as a present
by the Duke of Ts'in.   The last act shows us the end of the
sage's career and his death, which took place in 479 A. D.
His faithful disciple Tze Kung sees in a vision the pos-
thumous honors first bestowed upon Confucius by Kao Tî,
the founder of the Han dynasty, who ascended the throne
in 202 B. C.

The books of Confucius were proscribed, together with all
other literature except the writings on divination, agriculture
and medicine, by the order of She Hwang Tî[2], the founder of
the Ts'in dynasty, in the year 213 B. C., but the Ts'in dy-
nasty was of short duration.   Emperor Kao Tî and his suc-
cessors of the house of Han did their best to have the lost
treasures restored.   The emperor P'ing Tî had a temple erect-

2. She Hwang Tî was the first emperor to assume the title
Tî, implying the divine nature of a ruler's sovereign authority.
His name was Cheng and he is best known in history as the
builder of the great wall.   According to tradition he was the son
of the concubine of Chwang Siang Wang, the Duke of Ts'in, and
the latter's minister of state, Lü Pu Wei.   He ascended the throne
of Ts'in and subdued the other vassals of China, thus creating a
large empire and abolishing its feudal constitution.   Hence his
hostile attitude toward the ancient literature.   He was a man of
unusual ability and a ruler of indomitable energy, but hated by
the literati.   See William Frederick Mayers, *Chinese Reader's
Manual*, Part I, Nos. 465 and 597.

ed in the year 1 A. D., where sacrifices were offered to Confucius in company with the ancient model of virtue, Chow Kung. The titles under which the sage was revered changed slightly, but remained the same in spirit. They were "Illustrious Duke Ni," "Lord of Complete Praise," then "Prince of Illustrious Learning," "Sage of Antiquity," "Most Perfect Sage," etc. In the year 1743 the musical portion of Confucius worship was regulated by imperial decree in an elaborate style and, as we may assume, in a conservative fashion pretty nearly as represented in Tze Kung's vision at the conclusion of our drama.

*   *   *

The Chinese are an ethical nation. They love to ponder on ethics and in actual life are known to be unusually reliable. Western people who have dealings with the Chinese do not hesitate to characterize them as more trustworthy than members of other nations, and this is true not only of "big business" men but even of the cooly. As a rule Chinamen are praised for adhering to their contracts, even when rendered unfavorable by changed conditions.

The question now arises whether the Chinese have acquired their peculiar love of moralizing from their education which has come down to them from Confucius through two and a half millenniums, or whether Confucius has become acceptable to them as a teacher, as a national representative, because his doctrine comes nearest to the Chinese ideal. There may be truth in either proposition, for it is certain that we have to recognize Confucius as the representative type of Chinese manhood in China's classical past.

*   *   *

The essential elements of a tragedy consist in the endeavor of a man to stand up for his ideals. In doing so he offers himself and the best efforts of his life as a sacrifice for his conviction, and whether or not by his own fault suffers defeat in his personal interests, while from the wreckage of his life his ideals come out after his death in triumphant victory. In this sense we must grant that Confucius is a tragic figure. Confucius passed through all these stages and is now the

Christ of China, the divine revealer of truth, the teacher of right conduct. As Christ died in despair with the exclamation *Eli, Eli, lama sabachthani,* so Confucius ended in deep despondence with the words, "My teaching is finished." But after his death, when his mortal coil had been shuffled off and all personal ambition had been lost, his ideals were recognized, and as the representative of all moral aspirations he rose to the dignity of a superpersonal presence in the religious world-conception of his nation.

In the present drama we witness the growing enthusiasm of the disciples of Confucius and the spirit of comradeship among them that developed from their admiration for their master and his ideals. The personal ambition of Confucius to introduce his doctrines himself as a minister of state was only temporarily realized and he was compelled to retire into seclusion. For the rest of his life he tried in vain to be the leader, the teacher, the authorized adviser of some government. Possibly his personal ambition was a mistake. We are inclined to think that he should not have sought the official appointment of one of the rulers of his time; but even his intention to have his reforms introduced legally, by the sanction of some legitimate administration instead of by a revolution, was part of his scheme of moral ideals. He found no response while he lived, but after his death his fame spread all over China and later generations accepted his doctrines willingly. In spite of many defects in his philosophy and the justice of the criticism of his rival, Lao Tze, he was recognized as the official and legitimate revealer of morality.

Confucius has become the hero of all moral aspiration in China. But he is more; he incorporates the purely human. He is the man who in his own life followed the principle not to do unto others what he would not have others do to him. He represents the natural moral good-will which is a prominent feature in the life of humanity everywhere, and the present dramatic poem should be received in the sense of a tragedy describing the destiny which the moral hero must naturally encounter in ancient China or elsewhere.

CAST OF CHARACTERS

K'ung Fu Tze (Confucius).....................................*C*

Lady Ch'ien Kwan, Wife of Confucius....................*Lady C*

Niece of Confucius...*N*

Tze Kung, the faithful disciple...........................*Kung*

Ho Chi, called Mang-I, a prince of aristocratic appearance..*M.I.*

Chung Yû, styled Tze Lu, the courageous.....................*Lu*

Min Sun, styled Tze Ch'ien, orator and diplomat.............*Min*

Yen Hui, "Continuator of the Sage"; the favorite disciple, much younger than the others........................*Yen*

K'ung Lî, the son of Confucius..............................*Lî*

K'ung Chî, the grandson of Confucius, a boy of twelve years, later on famous as the author of "The Doctrine of the Mean" ....*Chî*

Tze Kao, a hunchback, of unusual brightness.................*Kao*

Li Erh, called Lao Tan or Lao Tze, the old philosopher, opposed to Confucius....................................*L. T.*

Lao Tan's attendant, a boy or half-grown youth.............*Boy*

Duke Ting, of the state of Lû.............................*Ting*

A native of Lo, the capital of the state Chow................*Lo*

An old man, displeased with his son.......................*O. M.*

A young man, sued by his father.............................*Son*

Liu Pang, emperor Kao Tî, founder of the Han dynasty and Institutor of Confucian worship; ascended the throne B. C. 202. Appears in Tze Kung's vision...............*Tî*

Bridesmaids, groomsmen, musicians and singing damsels.

ACT I.

SCENE I.

The Reception Room of Confucius in the year 518 B. C. In the background an entrance wide enough to show two persons outside. The door opens and two men, TZE KUNG *(Kung) and* MANG-I *(M. I.) are seen standing outside bowing to each other.*

Kung. Please enter, sir!

M. I.   I shall not be so rude
As to take precedence before my betters.

Kung. I am a simple man and your inferior;
E'en your deportment proves your higher rank.
Apparently you are of noble birth.
'Tis not your dress alone; I see quite plainly
You are accustomed to court etiquette,
While I am but a modest commoner.

M. I. Pray do not estimate my birth too high.
You are a gentleman of great distinction,
Of polished manners and accomplishments.

Kung. You are too kind in over-estimating
My worth. Oh, pray shame not your humble
    servant
By greater courtesy. Please enter first!

M. I. Let us step o'er the threshold both at once.

Kung. That would behoove me not. So please walk in,
And I will follow you. You are too kind.

M. I.   With your permission I will enter, then.

Kung.   Pray do so, sir.
              Mang-I *enters and* Tze Kung *follows.*
              And I will call the Master;
    But kindly tell me, sir, what kind of business
    Brings you to him. You are———?

M. I.   I am Ho Chi,
    Son of His Excellence, the late Mang Hsi,
    State Minister of Lû, and commonly
    Am called Mang-I.

Kung.   [*Bows low*] Mang-I! I'm greatly honored!
    I'm Twan Mu Tze and am addressed Tze Kung.
    I come from Wei and I take pride in being
    A pupil of the Master, K'ung Fu Tze.
    I know your honorable father died
    But a few weeks ago, and all the people
    Sincerely mourn his premature demise.
    He was a truly good and honest man,
    Rare in this troubled and degenerate age.

M. I.   [*Bows*] My father simply tried to do his duty;
    'Tis all that he accomplished since Duke Chao
    Appointed him his Minister of State.
    He knew, he said, that he was unprepared
    For his high duties. When he came to die
    He charged me to do better and to learn.
    "There is K'ung Ch'iu," he said, "a master sage
    Who's commonly addressed as K'ung Fu Tze.
    He dwelleth in this state of Lû, and he
    Knows more about our ancient institutions,
    About propriety and right and wrong,
    Than any living mortal, near or far.
    Go thou," my father said, "and learn from him."

Kung.   Blest be the memory of your dear father,
    For truly he was right in what he thought
    Of Master K'ung. Indeed K'ung is a sage.
    Some time ago I heard his knowledge praised

And went to him ambitious, proud and eager
To join at once our learned noble Master.

M. I.   How do you rank our K'ung Fu Tze as sage?

Kung.   I do not know, nor can I well describe it.
I've had the heavens all through my life o'er head,
But do not know their height.   I've had the earth
Beneath my feet, but do not know its depth.
I serve the Master, learn from him; his wisdom
Is infinite and inexhaustible!
I'm like a thirsty man who, with a pitcher,
Goes to the river's brink.   I draw the water
And drink my fill—pure water—yet know not
The river's depth and breadth and its supply.

M. I.   I envy thee, Tze Kung!   I fain would follow
This same good, noble Master, K'ung Fu Tze!

Kung.   And thee I welcome as a worthy comrade!
Thou art descended from a noble race,
And kin thou art to our own ducal house.

M. I.   Thou speakest truly, friend; my family
Is old and powerful, but princely birth
Does not confer a merit to be proud of.
It is the merit of mine ancestors,
Not of mine own, and I must live to earn it.
I only shall deserve my noble birth,
If I in thoughts and words and deeds prove noble,
If I excel in wisdom, truth and faith,
And if my soul be worthy of my rank.

Kung.   Such is the man I love!   Such is my Master;
For you may know perchance that K'ung Fu Tze
Traces descent from the imperial house
Of Yin.   His ancestor was Fu Fu Ho,
Best by his title known as the Duke Li,
The elder brother of Fang Sze; and Fu
Resigned the throne in favor of Fang Sze.

M. I.   I heard of it before but was not certain.

Kung.   Oh, if I were of noble family
Like unto K'ung or, sir, like unto you,
I would with all my power aspire to grow
Worthy the honor thus inherited.

M. I.   You are my friend, and, verily, he whom
His deeds have knighted is alone a knight.
Those who by noble birth are noble, are
But promises; they never shall be noble
Until they have redeemed their obligations.

> *Enter* CHUNG YÛ, *styled* TZE LU *(Lu), and* MIN
> SUN *(Min), styled* TZE CH'IEN, *both bowing
> to* MANG-I. KUNG *addresses the latter with
> dignity, by way of introduction.*

Kung.   Ho Chi, son of His Honor, the late Mang Hsi,
And styled Mang-I, here are the two disciples
Of our great master K'ung, whom I regard
As being most distinguished in our ranks.
You will be pleased to meet them, and the more
You know them both, the better you will like them.
Here is Min Sun, a dear good fellow student;
He is addressed Tze Ch'ien. And here's Chung Yû,
Known as Tze Lu and also called Chi-Lu.

M. I.   [*Addressing* MIN SUN, *standing nearest*]
Were you attracted by the Master's fame,
And did you come to profit by his wisdom?

Min.   An awkward country lad I hither came.

Kung.   But see, Mang-I, what K'ung Tze made of him.
He is an orator, a diplomat,
A man who has command of choicest speech;
Endowed he is with talent for persuasion.
Oh, it is wonderful how much he's changed!

Min.   Indeed it is, and all is K'ung Tze's work.

Kung.   Excuse me, sir, I'll go and call the Master.
I'll tell him of your presence and describe
The merits of his noble visitor.

M. I.   Pray, friend Tze Kung, do not exaggerate
The small accomplishments which I possess.
(Exit KUNG, *bowing to* MANG-I.*)*
[*To* MIN] Your home is in the rural districts, sir?

Min.   I came here from the midst of reeds and sedges
And joined the school of our revered great Master;
He trained my mind to filial piety,
Taught me the examples of the ancient kings—
And how I loved to be instructed! How
I loved to learn the wisdom of our sages!
But then another picture lured me on;
I saw the people in authority,
With all their pomp, their banners and umbrellas,
In gorgeous dress, surrounded by retainers.
I liked these shows, and yet I felt distressed,
Because the spectacles did not agree
With all that I had learned of justice, virtue
And of propriety. The Master's lessons,
However, have sunk deeply in my heart,
And the examples of my fellow students
Have also helped to set my mind at rest.
I see the emptiness of all the pomp,
And I regard it now no more than dust.
I value virtue now, virtue alone.
This solves for me all problems, and my mind
At last has found completest satisfaction.

M. I.   I know you follow the right master, sir.
The master that impressed you certainly
A paragon of wisdom is and virtue.
And what is your experience, Tze Lu? [*turning to*
TZE LU.]

Lu.   I sought the Master's good advice, and asked,
"What can you do for me? And how may I
Profit by you, your wisdom and your learning?"
Quoth he: "What love you best?" and I replied,
"I love my sword, my sharp and shining sword."
"Well," said the sage, "your stature and deportment

Bode courage. If you add a higher training
To your activities, you can become
Superior and a man of sterling worth."
That has from boyhood e'er been my ambition.
Thought I, superior men are born, not raised;
And so I ventured to object: "There grow
Some bamboo stalks here on the southern slope,
So straight that culture could not make them
    straighter;
Their fibers are so strong they pierce the hide
Of a rhinoceros."   And he, the Master,
Replied with calm composure: "It is true,
Superior men are born, yet even they
Need training. Aye! Your well-grown bamboo
    stalk
Can do far greater things if it be armed
With iron point and winged with feathers. Yea,
The arrow-maker chooses stalks both strong
And straight to make good arrows.   So the sage
Needeth disciples of good character."
That day I joined our learned, noble Master
And am convinced that I have found the man,
The only man who leadeth the right way.

M. I.   You are the man for me; let us be friends!
          The door opens. Enter CONFUCIUS *(C.) with*
          TZE KUNG.

Kung.   This is Mang-I, son of His Excellence,
          The late Prime Minister of State.

C.   Be seated,
          My noble sir, be seated.   Let me hear
          What I can do for you.

M. I.   My father, sir,
          In due appreciation of your wisdom,
          Charged me in his last will and testament
          To ask you for advice and kindly guidance,
          And bade me learn from you the principles

Of government, the standard and the rules
Both of good conduct and propriety.
But above all, I need a thorough knowledge
Of ancient ceremonies and of rites
Sorely neglected in our present day.

C.   I shall do all I can for you, dear sir,
The principles are easy—application,
The details and the practice difficult.

M. I.   I humbly beg your pardon, honored sir;
I am no scholar, nor a sage like you.
I find the practice frequently quite easy.
I know how to conduct and bear myself;
It seems to come to me like second nature.
The principle alone 'tis puzzles me.

C.   Nature has made this world relational,
There are two opposites, the Yang and Yin,
Which show themselves in their peculiar mixtures
Throughout creation: be it as sun and moon,
As earth and heaven, as female and as male,
As light and darkness, or as day and night,
As positive and negative; and man,
You know it well, is mixed of earth and heaven.
All is relational in human life,
And there are five relations, all ordained
In laws of nature between Yang and Yin.
Yang is the strong and lordly part, the mover;
Yin, being womanly and meek, endureth.
There's the relation between prince and subject,
Between a father and his son; and thirdly,
Between the elder and the younger brother;
Fourthly, between the husband and his wife;
And fifth and lastly, between a friend and friend.

M. I.   Blest be this lucky day on which I met you;
But pray, dear Master, how must I proceed
To profit, to advance, to learn from you?

C.   I see that you are vigorous and manly,
          Your gait and stature bode both strength and
            courage.

Lu.   Sir, he reminds me of our former talk,
          He's like the bamboo on the southern hill
          Which grows up straight and has no nick nor bent,
          So straight that culture could not make it straighter.

C.   But culture can improve on nature's work.

M. I.   Your words indeed are true, and I will learn
          The lessons that you teach. You'll find me ready
          To accept instruction with due reverence.
          Before I leave, sir, may I be permitted
          To ask a special favor?

C.   Speak, and I
          Will do whatever lies within my power.

M. I.   The ancient capital of our great empire
          Is many-peopled Lo.   The customs there
          And rites are still observed in purest form.
          The ruler, being of the house of Chow,
          Is emperor at least in name, and there
          The archives are; there is the library
          Which holds the choicest lore of former ages,
          The temple services are there retained
          Now as in olden times, and there at court
          The ceremonies are most dignified.
          Would you, great Master, undertake a journey
          To Lo, the seat of deepest thought and learning,
          And introduce me to its wondrous treasures?

C.   I will, dear sir; and thou shalt be to me
          As mine own son, to whom I shall bequeathe
          The deepest words of wisdom I have found.

M. I.   Our gracious overlord, the Duke of Lû,
          Is well acquainted with my father's wish;
          He has approved of it, and biddeth me
          To send his royal greetings to your Honor.

He says that he will speed the voyage by
Equipping you with carriage and good horses.
He'll give you letters to His Majesty
The Emperor, which will prepare for you
A dignified reception, and will open
To you the temples and the archives.

C.   Welcome,
Most welcome, is this offer, friend Mang-I,
And most auspicious shall this journey prove.
In Lo there lives Li Erh, a famous sage
Called Lao Küen, also Lao Tan
Or Lao Tze, the old philosopher,
The venerable keeper of the archives.
He sees the urgent need of a reform
And he will help us in our enterprise.
He'll smooth our paths, and his authority
Will be of greatest service to our cause.

SCENE II.

Courtyard in the House of Confucius. *From the
door on the right the* NIECE *of Confucius (N.)
peeps out, looking expectantly toward the door
in the center. She withdraws quickly. The
door in the center opens and* LU *leads out*
MANG-I. *The two walk out toward the right
when the lady comes out and passes them.*
MANG-I, *stepping aside to make room for her,
bows low and reverently; she acknowledges the
salutation by a slight but dignified motion of her
head and disappears in the house.*

M. I.   Pray tell me, my friend Lu, who is this lady?

Lu.   She is the niece of our great Master, K'ung.

M. I.   I might have thought she is some kin to him—
So stately and superior, a true lady.
Forsooth, it can be seen that K'ung Fu Tze

A scion is of an imperial line;
Whatever is connected with the sage
Beareth the stamp of royalty.

Lu.   You know
He has descended from the house of Yin
That held the empire for six centuries
And more, until Chow Sin, the unworthy tyrant,
The last one of his race upon the throne,
Was vanquished by Wu Wang, the war king, Fa,
The founder of the present dynasty,
The house of Chow which now the empire holds.

M. I.   This house rules but in name. It has no power,
For every prince does as it pleases him.
The barons are no better; nor are they
In turn submissive to the dukes, their princes,
And the result is chaos—needing reform.

Lu.   Yea, from the chaos suffers all the world.
Our wise and able Master tries reform,
And a reform he surely will achieve.

SCENE III.

The Women's Apartment in Confucius' House.
LADY CHIEN KWAN *(L. C.), the wife of Con-
fucius, and his* NIECE *(N.) are seen engaged in
sewing.*

N.   Auntie, Aunt Chien, is it wrong to look at a man?

L. C.   What do you mean, dearie? You didn't look at a
man, did you? [*Looking at the girl with a serious ex-
pression of reproof.*]
          [NIECE *nods with a roguish smile of admission.*]
And who was it?

N.   I don't know. He was a stranger. He must have
been visiting uncle. Oh, he was a man! A real
man.

L. C.   You met him?
          [*N. nods again.*]
          I hope it was by accident?

N.   Certainly, it was the sheerest accident. He came
          through the gate when I looked up from my em-
          broidery and gazed through the window. He
          couldn't see me. He was hardly like a man.

L. C.   You called him just now a real man.

N.   Oh, yes, a real man. He is manly but he looked
          more than a man.

L. C.   Like a gentleman?

N.   Oh, much more! There was something superior
          about him. [*Musing*] You know, auntie, if I
          were a sculptor I would carve Kwang Tî, the great
          God, the war-lord, like him. I wonder who he was.
          Really, auntie, I am not curious, but perhaps you
          could ask uncle who his visitor was?

L. C.   What an improper suggestion! Uncle would be
          indignant to learn of your inquisitiveness.

N.   Would he? Oh, I don't mean anything improper,
          I only wished to know something about him. You
          see, he might inquire about me.

L. C.   How could he, child? He didn't see you.

N.   Oh, yes, he did. [*After a pause*] You see, while
          I looked out of the window, Tze Lu met him.
          The two walked together and went to the house to
          uncle. I watched the door because—well, because
          I wondered—because he stayed so long.

L. C.   My child, I am alarmed. I have never noticed in
          your behavior a lack of propriety and I must say that
          this is—to say the least—not becoming in a girl of
          good family. How can you take any interest in a
          strange man!

N. I took no interest in the stranger. I was only interested in uncle, and wondered what the stranger had to say to him and what uncle might think of the stranger. Can't I be interested in uncle?

L. C. Oh, certainly, in uncle, but you say the stranger saw you. How did that happen?

N. Well, auntie, that was another accident. You see, I needed some more silk skeins. I have enough red and pink silk, but I need orange. The stranger wore a scarf of deep orange and I wanted a skein of that color, and it must be exactly *that* color, for no other will do. So I went to call the nurse to send her to the merchant, but she had to see the scarf. I called the nurse and couldn't find her; and then I went out into the courtyard, thinking that I would find the girl over there in the kitchen. I was a little afraid that the stranger would cross the yard and so I waited a little and watched the door. Well, I don't say exactly that I was afraid of meeting the stranger but I tried to avoid him; but just when I crossed the courtyard the door opened and he saw me. That is why I wanted to ask you if it is wrong to look at a man. I was in an awful position. You can't realize, auntie, how awful it was.

L. C. You poor child, you should not have ventured into the yard.

N. Now you see; he looked at me and stood still only for a moment, gazing at me as if in a dream, then he bowed low and passed out of the gate.

L. C. I hope you didn't look at him?

N. Oh, no, I only took a quick peep at him, but he looked at me.

L. C. You should not have raised your eyes even for a second.

N. How could I help it? He was so courteous and
    so respectful,—and he was so manly! You should
    have seen him. I had scarcely time to note the color
    of his scarf. That scarf was fine, and only for the
    sake of the scarf I should like to know who he was.

L. C. My dear child, I must reprove you for your be-
    havior; and I expect of you most decidedly that such
    scenes shall not occur again.

N. But, auntie, it was all an accident. I couldn't help it.

L. C. My dear, that is all very well, but I have the im-
    pression that you stand in need of advice. You are
    no longer a child. The time has come when you
    must be watchful and guarded in your conduct. Let
    virtue and honor be always your first consideration.
    Avoid even the mere semblance of impropriety.
    Even the thought of a man must never rise in your
    mind. You have made a series of mistakes. First,
    you should not have looked up from your embroid-
    ery; second, you should not have looked out of the
    window; third, if a man entered the gate you should
    not have beheld him at all. Then you should not
    have thought of him as being a man. Oh, and how
    dreadful it was to go out where you could meet him!

N. But, auntie, he didn't look dangerous. I am sure
    he is a gentleman and he looked like a prince. He
    must have been a nobleman. His dress, his gait, his
    carriage were distinguished and he was as beautiful
    as a young god. I loved the very sight of him. Oh,
    auntie, I wish you had seen him, you would have
    liked him, too. I'm sure there is no one in all the
    Middle Kingdom so manly and so lordlike as this
    mysterious stranger.

L. C. Child, my wayward child! What is the matter
    with you? You speak as if you were in love. Calm
    yourself. You are infatuated with a vision.

N.   In love? Is that possible?

L. C. Forget the stranger and learn the rules of modesty
and propriety. A young girl like you must not allow
her heart to be carried away. You are young and
inexperienced, and do not know the dangers of the
world.

N.   Teach me, auntie, I will be glad to learn.

L. C. Look here, my good niece, this is the picture of your
grandmother. She was Lady K'ung, the mother
of your uncle K'ung Fu Tze, and she indeed was
worthy to become the mother of a great sage.
Grandfather K'ung was a mighty man and a general
of renown. He had been married to a lady who
bore him nine daughters and no son. How he
longed for an heir who could perform the proper
ritual sacrifices at his tomb! So he went to his
friend, the honorable Yen, a man of distinction, and
asked him for one of his daughters in marriage.
The Honorable Mr. Yen addressed his three daugh-
ters and said: "Is there one of you who will marry
General K'ung? He has been a courageous soldier
and stood the brunt of many a fight in the service of
the Duke of Lû. In his best years he was strong
and tall. He still stands over ten shoes in height,
but he has grown old and counts now eighty years."
Mr. Yen then asked his oldest daughter, "Would
you take him for a husband?" but she cherished in
her heart the image of another man who was fair
to look upon, and said: "I feel myself honored by
General K'ung's proposal but I prefer to have my
own choice." The second daughter answered: "If
I marry General K'ung I shall have to be a nurse
all my wedded life. Instead of having a husband
I should have a patient on my hands. Pray let the
general take some one else for wife, some one who
would like to become a young widow." When Mr.

Yen turned to his youngest daughter, she replied, "Father, do with me as thou thinkest best. I will be thy obedient child." And the father rejoiced, saying: "Thou art a fit bride for the general. Mayst thou bear him a son worthy of the noble K'ung family." Her son is K'ung Tze! A woman must be humble and submissive, and especially before her marriage she should be demure and modest.

N.   That is very good. And really I will be modest and humble; I admire all the virtues, but I care little for obedience. I will be obedient and marry any-body whom you or uncle wish, provided it is the man I love, and I want to look up to my husband as my lord. But he must be lordlike and of course [*in a peevish tone*] he must treat me as his lady. You do not mean a wife to be the slave of her hus-band? If the rules of propriety mean complete sub-mission to some old shaky invalid, I would rather not marry at all.

L. C.   What do you say, my child? You speak not as it behooves the granddaughter of the noble General K'ung. I must reprimand you most severely.

N.   Oh, dearest aunt, do not blame me. Consider your-self and the sad fate of all women. We are not allowed to be ourselves. We have no choice. Our lot is to be obedient. First, we must obey our parents, then our husbands. We have no rights ourselves, and happy is our lot if our husbands are half-way worthy of our attention and accept our services with kindly recognition. You know, auntie, what I wish? I want a husband whom I love, and he must love me—or I would not care for him.

L. C.   You wayward child. You do not know enough of life, and you dream too much. I fear there are sad disappointments in store for you.

N.   Then let me have my dreams as long as cruel reality
has not yet destroyed them.

           Enter Confucius.   Lady C. *kneels down, so does
his* Niece, *the latter with some hesitation.*

L. C.   My husband and my lord!

C.   Rise, my good wife.
Rise to your feet and hear the important news!
In company with Lu, Kung and Mang-I,
The son of the late Minister of State,
I go to visit Lo, the ancient city
And whilom capital of our great country,
The venerable center of our culture,
Where lives the greatest of philosophers,
The noble, venerable Lao Tan.
And there I shall imbibe at its first source
Hoary traditions of our history
And knowledge of the great men of the past.
All shall be utilized for a reform
Of this decadent nation, and the future
Will be as bright and glorious as great Yü
And Shao and Wu Wang could ever make it.
I will revive the virtue of the ancients
And I shall be the leader in reform!
My star is rising, nevermore to set.

                   (Curtain.)

ACT II.

SCENE I.

*The Hall of Light in the City of Lo, in the year
518. The imperial throne-room of the house of
Chow decorated in a gorgeous old Chinese style.
Behind the elevated throne a picture of the Duke
of Chow with his infant nephew. Enter Con-
FUCIUS with his disciples.*

M. I.   This is a place which I have longed to see.
How beautiful it is and full of relics,
Of sacred symbols, ancient art and pictures.

C.   It is the Hall of Light, the venerable
Old throne-room of the imperial house of Chow.
Here is a lesson.   We cannot understand
The present age unless we know the past!
The last one of the house of Yin, Chow Sin,
Is known as tyrant and his crimes are many.
We owe our father love and reverence,
We owe allegiance to our sovereign, but
Such rights imply great duties, and if duties
Are heedlessly neglected, heaven will punish
The trespassers!   So Heaven dealt with Yin.
A sovereign's, as a father's, rights depend
Upon his goodness; if he lacks true goodness,
He surely forfeits his authority.
Si Pêh, named Ch'ang, Chief of the West, Wen
    Wang,
Had suffered much abuse, was cast in prison
By Sin, the tyrant, and in tribulation
Found comfort only in the Book of Yih,

The sacred permutations which divined
For him a glorious triumph of his cause,
And truly, he regained his liberty.
Then after him his valiant son Wu Wang
With the assistance of some other princes
O'erthrew the debauched tyrant in pitched battle.
And thereupon the tyrant lost his realm,
Wu Wang ascended the imperial throne
As founder of the dynasty of Chow.
See here above the royal seat portrayed
The Duke of Chow, a brother of Wu Wang,
Holding aloft the infant emperor,
Named Ch'ang, the heir apparent to the realm.
Wu Wang had died and left a minor son,
Ward of his faithful brother, Duke of Chow.
The Duke might easily have set himself
Upon his much lamented brother's throne,
But he would not deprive his orphaned nephew
Of his inheritance.   He kept the trust,
And here you see this noble, honest man!
The vassals of the empire swear allegiance
To their child emperor whose rights he shielded.
See here the secret basis of Chow's greatness!
Justice alone can make an empire strong;
Where justice lacks, decay is not far off.

M. I.   Sir, wonderful is this, and history
Is full of lessons!   You expound them well.
And from the past we learn the principles
By which the future should be guided.

C.   Friends,
Our culture is much older than the Yin.
Here are the first five rulers of our realm:
Here is Fu Hi, the oldest of them all,
Who lived more than two thousand years ago
In ages of remote antiquity.
Here are his diagrams, eight combinations
Of whole and broken lines, of Yang and Yin,

Of positive and negative, developed
From the primordial unit, T'ai Chih,
The absolute containing in itself
Duality.   Here is Fu Hi's successor,
Shên Nung She, inventor of the plow.
Hwang Ti, the yellow emperor, gave us
The calendar and built the first great temple
Wherein to worship God, the Lord on High.
He was a master in philosophy,
Extending the eight trigrams of Fu Hi
Into the four and sixty hexagrams.
His wife, Si Ling, taught us to rear the silkworm.
Yao the great and Shun laid the foundation
Of great prosperity; they regulated
The river courses, thus preventing floods,
And it was Yü the Great who built the dykes.
Shao did not appoint his son successor,
He did not deem him worthy of the honor;
He chose the humble Shun of lowly birth,
Distinguished by his filial piety.
And filial piety is bottom rock,
The bottom rock on which we build our culture
Whose application lies in five relations,
And five ideals stand out paramount:
Humaneness, uprightness, propriety,
Enlightenment, and, last not least, good faith.
Here we have seen the treasures of the past,
But higher still than art and precious relics
We deem the learning of the sage, for he
Can teach us wisdom, truth and also virtue.
The greatest mind that now our country holds
Is Lao Tan, the old philosopher;
And you and I shall see him face to face.

SCENE II.

The Archives of Chow in the city Lo.   LAO TAN
*(L. T.), a man of advanced years with a flowing
white beard, is seated at a table with a lute before
him.*

L. T. The reason that can be reasoned is not the eternal reason. The word that can be spoken is not the eternal word. The reason that can be reasoned is man's reason. Man's reason is vain and subject to error. I long for the eternal reason, the reason of Heaven. Heaven's reason is unnamable. It is the mother of the world, the mother of the ten thousand things. We call it Tao. Man's reason is but a faint echo of the Tao. Man imagines, however, that his human and all too human reason is unfailing. The genuine human reason and the heavenly reason are truly one and the same. I long for the eternal reason, the Tao. She is my mother, I am her child. But to be the son of the eternal reason, I must have no reason of my own; no reason in contradiction to the Tao, the heavenly reason. I must empty my heart of desire.

> *He begins to play the lute and sings in a melo-dramatic strain*:

> He who desireless is found
> The spiritual of the world will sound;
> But he who by desire is bound
> Sees the mere shell of things around.

> *Boy enters and makes a bow. He waits respectfully until* LAO TAN *stops playing, then bows again.* LAO TAN *looks up expectantly.*

Boy. K'ung Chin of the State of Lû, attended by Tze Lu, Tze Kung and Mang-I, the son of His Excellence Mang Hsi, late Minister of Lu, are here to pay you their respects.

L. T. Who is K'ung Chin? Is it K'ung Tze, the modern sage of Lû, who would fain reform the whole world by reviving the past? [*Boy hands him a slip of paper bearing the name of K'ung Fu Tze.* LAO TAN *reads it*] Indeed, that is the man. It is

K'ung Tze with some of his disciples. Let him enter.

Boy bows and goes out.

L. T. [*Speaking to himself*] He is gaining fame and people praise him; yet it seems to me that he clings to externalities. [*Lets his fingers run over his lute again*] He preaches virtue; he proclaims justice; he insists on ceremonial, the ceremonial of the past, the old dead past. The great reason, the ineffable, inexpressible reason is not so complicated. Does K'ung know its simplicity? I fear he is far from it. What we need is singleness of heart.

Accompanying himself on the lute, Lao Tan sings again:

The simplicity of the unexpressed
Will purify the heart of lust.
Where there's no lust, there will be rest,
And all the world will thus be blest.

The great Tao, the eternal reason, is as if non-existent. It is as empty as the expanse of heaven but its use is inexhaustible.

Confucius *and his disciples enter with conspicuous dignity.*

C. Blest be our entrance here where holy scrolls
Greet us from all the shelves. These curious writings
Come from the hands of our ancestral sages.
The hoary past is speaking unto us
Here in these archives of old emperors.
Yea, enviable is thy fate, great Lao Tan,
Curator of the holy scriptures here!

Lao Tan *has risen and the two sages bow repeatedly.*

L. T. If I can help thee, worthy guest, command me.

C.   O noble Lao Tan, thy wisdom is
Well known through all the empire. Kindly, sir,
Let us reap benefits from thy great knowledge.
Most wondrous the resources thou hast here
In these famed archives of the House of Chow,
Which since the day of Wu has ruled the country.
There may be documents in thy possession
That date as far back as the house of Yin;
Yea, traces may be here among thy treasures
Of the primordial founders of our land,
Of the five ancient rulers; of Fu Hi,
Inventor of our script; of Sheng Nung She,
The godly husbandman who taught the people
To fashion plows from wood; further Hwang Ti
The yellow emperor, or one of his
Six ministers; perhaps some other sages
Have left some record of our ancient rites.

L. T.   The men of whom you speak, sir, all are dead,
And now are mouldering in their graves. Their
    words
Alone are extant still. 'Tis of no use
To see the places where they lived, to handle
The manuscripts they wrote with their own hands
Simply for us to make a show of learning.

C.   Allow me to insist that all the rulers
Should make a show of their authority,
And their authority is based upon
The wisdom of tradition, of the past.
The people ought to see that they are governed.

L. T.   No, sir. I differ from you on this point.
The people scarcely knew of the existence
Of our great rulers. Lesser ones they liked
And praised. Still lesser ones they feared, and then
The least, the meanest, smallest they despised.

C.   No, sir, oh no!

L. T.   Yes, sir, they still despise them.

C. Rulers must seek advice from noble sages,
Must recognize their worth. Should not the sage
Stand high exalted? He should be distinguished,
And monarchs should surround themselves with
  sages.

L. T. The sage should imitate the eternal reason,
The great Tao which makes all things arise.
What would you do if you were called to rule?

C. I would establish righteousness and justice,
Would make the ruler truly be a ruler,
The subject be a subject, would reform
The empire, would convert the world to virtue,
And I would do, in short, what should be done.

L. T. [*After a short pause, ironically*]
You would, indeed, make much ado. You would
Make a great show of virtue and assert
Your principle.

C.   Sir, what else should I do?

L. T. What should you do, you ask? Do no ado!
Do not assert yourself. Does heaven e'er
Assert itself? But heaven for aye endures;
Your person put behind, for only thus
Cometh your person to the fore. The sage
Will never boast of his own worth. He quickens
But does not own; he works but does not claim;
Merit he gains, but does not dwell on it.

C. The sage should set the people an example
Of justice, of benevolence, and virtue.

L. T. Of virtue? Sir, it seems you mean the sage
To make a show of virtue; 'twere but sham.
True virtue knoweth naught of show or sham.
True virtue is unvirtue, not ado.
If goodness makes a show of goodness, sir,
It is sheer badness and hypocrisy.

Further, if beauty makes display of beauty,
It is sheer ugliness, to be despised.
When people lose the Tao, virtue comes;
Then they begin to talk and preach of virtue.
If they lose virtue, then benevolence
Comes in its place.   They lose benevolence
And justice comes.   When they lose justice, too,
They preach propriety.   Propriety
Is but a semblance of true loyalty,
Of goodness, virtue, faith.   This hankering
After traditions old, this reverence
Of virtue, justice and benevolence
Is a mere empty show which but conceals
The lack of reason and of genuine virtue.
It is the flower of reason, not its fruit.

C.   You undervalue what the sage can do
If he but finds the place which he deserves.

L. T.   A noble man who finds his time, will rise;
But if he does not find his time, he drifts,
And like a roving plant he'll have to wander.
Let go, sir, your ambitious affectation,
Your haughty airs.   All this is of no use.

C.   Sir, you are frank!

L. T.   Truthful you'd have me be.
True words, sir, are not pleasant; pleasant words
Are scarcely true.

C.   You are discouraging.

L. T.   Do I discourage when I would correct?
I'd but discourage him who seeketh self;
Not him who seeketh Tao and would find it.
I seek the Tao, and the Tao, sir,
Serves me as guide.   It is the middle path
Between extremes and leads us to the goal.
The Tao teaches virtue, teaches goodness,
And all we need is goodness.

C.   Goodness only?

L. T.   Meet all with goodness; meet the good with goodness
           And likewise, too, meet evil ones with goodness.

C.   My principle is justice.   Do not to others
           What thou wouldst not have done to thee.   Indeed
           The good ones we should meet with goodness, truly!
           But bad ones I would meet as they deserve.
           For why should we the bad ones also treat
           With goodness, say?   The words which thou hast
              spoken,
           Are hard to understand.
           (*As if speaking to himself*:)
                                   Oh, I had hoped
           To learn from thee of ancient rituals,
           Of ceremonials and propriety!

L. T.   For all of which I care so little, sir!
           So let that go.   I have no more to say.

C.   Then we will part, and I for one regret
           That from thy wisdom I could learn no more.

           Both rise and bow, and LAO TAN *accompanies*
           CONFUCIUS *to the door.   Exit* CONFUCIUS, *ac-*
           companied by MANG-I, TZE LU *and* TZE
           KUNG.

L. T.   So that was K'ung Fu Tze, the great reformer?
           Is he the herald of a sterile future?
           Will he build up our nation?   Woe to us!
           Or am I so mistaken in the truth?
           There is a gulf 'twixt us cannot be bridged.
           Would he might find the Tao, but its light
           Shineth in vain; he comprehends it not.

           (*He begins to muse.*)
           How few there are who understand the Tao!
           We look at it and yet we see it not;
           We listen for its voice but hear no sound;
           We grope for it but cannot touch its form;

Yet it exists, it moulds this whole grand world.
It is a being wondrous and complete;
Ere heaven and earth, IT was. How calm it is!
Alone it standeth and it suffereth not,
Therefore it is the mother of the world.
I do not know its name—I call it Tao.
K'ung meaneth well, but will with failure meet;
He cannot find his time and he will drift
From place to place in idle quest. And I?
And I? I am forlorn, Oh, so forlorn!
I am a stranger here; I long for home.
My days are numbered and I will depart.
Yes, Yes! Abroad in life and home in death!

SCENE III.

A Street in Lo, the capital of Chow. *Enter a native of Lo (Lo).* CONFUCIUS *passes by. He appears disconcerted and agitated as if he had lost his way. Exit* CONFUCIUS. *Native of Lo looks back after* CONFUCIUS, *shakes his head and expresses astonishment.*

Lo.   A remarkable man! I wonder who he is? A striking figure!

Enter MANG-I, TZE LU *and* TZE KUNG.

Lu.   Sir, have you seen a stranger here?

Lo.   Yes, sir, I have.

Lu.   Perhaps it was the Master, K'ung Fu Tze.
Did he appear to you extraordinary?

Lo.   Indeed he did, sir. The man I saw had a forehead like Yâo, the wise emperor; a neck like Kao Yâo, the great minister of Shun; shoulders much like Ts'ze-Ch'an, who governed Cheng so well in times of great disorder! He wanted a little below the waist of the height of Yü the Great, the builder of our dykes. Indeed, an extraordinary man, but his general demeanor was that of a stray dog.

Lu.   That is our Master; we have found him.

Kung. Whither did he go?

Lo.   There he comes now.
         Enter CONFUCIUS

Kung. O Master, venerable Master! At last we found you.

M. I. We were much worried and have searched for you.

C.   O friends, I'm disconcerted, and I feel
         Defeated and dejected since I met
         The ancient sage, the famous Lao Tan.

M. I. You have no reason to be thus downcast.
         With all due reverence for Lao Tan
         I think that he but failed to understand;
         May be that he at bottom means the same.

C.   I know the birds can fly, and fishes swim;
         I know wild beasts can run.   But man devises
         Snares for the runner, nets to catch the swimmer
         And with his arrows brings the flyers down.
         I know it, but the dragon I know not.
         The dragon is miraculous and grand;
         The dragon can bestride the wind and clouds
         When rising heavenward.   I know him not.
         This Lao Tan, methinks, is like the dragon.

M. I. Be not discomfitted, my dear, good Master, .
         E'en though your views do not agree with Tan's
         You have an aim, a noble aim.   You will
         Accomplish something in this world.   And I
         Will stand by you.

Kung.   Pursue your aim, dear Master,
         We will stand by you, and we shall not flinch.

M. I. We will be faithful to the very end.

C.   I thank you from the bottom of my heart.
         You both are faithful, and you both are manly.
         Since you've been with me, Kung, I have no longer
         Seen sneers in faces of unfriendly people

Who would not countenance my thought.   But here
Against the great philosopher Lao Tan
You are of no avail.   Mang-I, you, too,
Have proved a help, but all your influence
Will not win the support of this lone thinker
For our great, noble cause.

M. I.   My dear good Master,
I have such faith in you I cannot see
How you can feel so grievously dejected
Merely because one dreamy simpleton
As old as he is singular and hazy
And odd, differs from you.   Leave him alone.
If he or any one of his admirers
Would venture to oppose us, let them do so.
We need opponents and we'll meet them squarely.
Your mission 'tis to rear the eternal pillars
Of the good doctrine, of propriety,
The golden rule, the five relationships.

C.   I thank you, my good friends, most cordially.

Kung.   Not for ourselves alone, we speak for all
Your followers and for your true disciples.

M. I.   We will convert the world to you.   And, Master,
[*With some hesitation*]   I wish to be allied to you
     and to
Your family.   Kindly allow me, sir,
To send to you as soon as we reach home,
A go-between who would arrange my marriage
To your fair niece.

C.   My niece?

M. I.   Yea, to your niece.

C.   My niece to me is like unto a daughter,
And no one, friend Mang-I, would be more welcome
As son-in-law than you.   Your cheering word,
Most noble sir, shall be a prophecy
Of the great future which before me lies.

ACT III.

SCENE I.

Home of Confucius, in the year 517 B. C. NIECE *of Confucius is seen in festive bridal attire, attended by maids.*

N.   The day is come, and here I wait for him;
And oh, to look upon him—to behold
His manly figure and his kindly face.
Hand me my lute and I will sing the song
My uncle taught me, the old bridal song
That has come down to us from hoary ages
And which exactly fits my present mood.

A maid hands her a lute. She plays and sings:

At the gate awaits me now,
    Screened from sight, hi-ho!
One with tassels o'er his brow
    All of white, hi-ho!
Gems beam bright!
What a sight! Hi-ho!

Through the courtyard now he goes
    Past the screen. Hi-ho!
Jewels which his headgear shows
    Are of green, hi-ho!
Such a sheen
Is rarely seen. Hi-ho!

He approaches now the hall,
    I am told; Hi-ho!

'Tis my bridegroom, among all
    Fair to b'hold.   Hi-ho!
Decked with gold,
Fair to behold.   Hi-ho!*

Enter CONFUCIUS *and his wife.*

C.   My dearest niece, no fault has yet been made.
The go-between has come and we've transacted
All details as prescribed by ancient custom.
Your names and ages have been stated; presents
Have been exchanged and our consent is given;
The day of marriage has been duly fixed.
And we await thy bridegroom, now to take thee
Home to his parents' house, yea, to their palace,
For they are wealthy and of royal blood.
Thy mother-in-law expects thee, with desire
To have thee with her, for she loves thee dearly,
The bride of her beloved and favorite son.

Maid.   The groom is coming; the procession neareth;
Mang-I is gorgeous as Kwang Ti himself,
Surrounded by his relatives and friends.

C.   [*To the servant*]   Show the musicians in, and call
        the maids.

*Enter musicians and a group of girls.   The former
with their instruments take seats on the right;
the latter surround the bride.   The table with
the lute is removed and a palanquin is brought.*

C.   Is the trousseau in readiness?

L. C.   It is.
Here are the boxes packed with proper care.
    [*Turning to her niece*]
Oh, my dear niece, how happy is your lot,

---

* This song is a translation of "The Bride's Ditty" in the Shî
King (I, VIII, 3), the poetical classic, collected and edited by
Confucius.

That just the man to whom your heart went out
Asked you in marriage.   This is rare, my child.

The door opens.   Enter MANG-I, *followed by a
procession.   The music plays.* MANG-I *bows
to* CONFUCIUS, *his wife and the bride.*

C.   [*To Mang-I*]
My friend, this is a day of purest joy.
Thou wilt the husband be of this my niece,
A maiden pure and undefiled, a treasure
In education and accomplishments
As well as noble in descent.   She will
Obedient and submissive prove to thee
As it behooves a wife; and thou, my friend,
Wilt prove her lord, her husband, her protector.
This day is most auspicious.   'Tis to be
The luckiest of the lucky days of life.
With this my wish, friend Mang-I, take her home.
Be happy with her; do thou make her happy;
Be happy both, according to your love.

*The music begins; the groomsmen and bridesmaids
lead the bridegroom to the bride, whom he con-
ducts with ceremonious courtesy to the palanquin.
All the attendants join in singing the ditty on
"The Locusts"* from the Shî King I, I, 5.   Our
translation is by William Jennings.*

How do the locusts crowd—
    A fluttering throng!
May thy descendants be
    Thus vast, thus strong!

How do the locusts' wings
    In motion sound!
May thy descendants show,
    Like them, no bound!

* The locust is an emblem of prowess in China.   See *The Open
Court* for January, 1913, pp. 57-61.

How do the locusts all
    Together cluster!
May thy descendants, too,
    In such wise muster!

While the bride is carried out in the palanquin, they
sing the "Bridal Song," from the Shî King I, I, 6.
Our translation is by William Jennings.

Ho, graceful little peach-tree,
    Brightly thy blossoms bloom!
The maid goes to her husband;
    Adorns his hall, his room.

Ho, graceful little peach-tree,
    Thy fruit abundant fall!
The maid goes to her husband;
    Adorns his room, his hall.

Ho, graceful little peach-tree,
    With foliage far and wide!
The maid goes to her husband;
    His household well to guide.

Exeunt all except CONFUCIUS *and* LADY C.

C.   A happy day this is for me. The marriage
Of Mang to our good niece can only serve
To make him even more attached to me
Than ever; and I prize his friendship high.
This morning only have I summoned been
To call on our most gracious lord, Duke Ting,
Who seeks my service. I am called upon
To govern first a district, then the state.
Here is my chance; I shall make use of it.

L. C.   Our lord Duke Ting is young and pleasure loving;
He is not constant, and success is doubtful.
I do not trust the honor beckoning thee.

C.　　Wife, have no doubt, for in my inmost soul
　　　I feel that Providence selected me
　　　To carry out the great plan of reform.
　　　There is no one on earth except myself
　　　Who knows the needs of mankind, who can teach
　　　The rules of conduct, who can regulate
　　　The five relations, and I feel convinced
　　　The Lord on High will speed me with success.
　　　When I was young I was in office twice.
　　　First I was keeper of the stores of grain,
　　　Then I had charge of public fields and land.
　　　Both offices were humble, certainly,
　　　But I was faithful in these smaller duties.
　　　My calculations balanced and the cattle
　　　Under my care did prosper.　Madam, then
　　　Do you remember when our son was born
　　　The Duke sent me a present of two carp—
　　　It was the father of the young Duke Ting—
　　　In friendly recognition of my work.
　　　I shall be just as faithful now in this,
　　　My new position, with its wider range.
　　　It is the cause of heaven I advocate,
　　　The cause of heaven cannot be doomed to failure.

ACT IV.

SCENE I.

Twenty Years Later. Court of the State Lû, in
497. *In the background the judgment seat with
a screen behind. In the foreground* YEN HUI
(Yen), TZE KUNG *and* TZE LU.

Lu. [*To* YEN] There was a time when I was jealous, sir,
Jealous of you for our great Master's love.
But you have overcome all my ill-feeling.
For, to be frank, I love you too.

Kung. And you
Are worthy to be cherished by us all,
You are so thoughtful, gentle, lovable.
The Master loves you, and who loves you not?

Yen. O, do not praise me, I do not deserve it.
I love the Master and I cannot help it.
I loved him as a child. My father loved him.
My father being one of his disciples
Looked up to him with deepest reverence.
And I was born to this my father's spirit,
In deepest reverence for the Master, K'ung.
I have imbibed it with my mother's milk
And was brought up in this same atmosphere.
When I grew older and began to think
I saw good reason for admiring him.
Who is the safest guide for all the world.

Unnoticed by the others, K'UNG Lî *(Li), the son
of Confucius, enters and listens.*

Lu.　And you are right, my friend, my dear Yen Hui.
　　　The Master showed for me consideration;
　　　He often followed my advice, and I
　　　Was near to him, nearer than all the others;
　　　But since you came and joined our company
　　　You have become nearest of all, and he
　　　Looketh to you to carry on his work.
　　　'Tis you whom he regards as his successor.

Kung.　He loves you more than his own son, and I
　　　Gladly confess that you deserve his favor.

Li.　[*Aside*] 'Tis true, my father loves him more than
　　　　me.

Yen.　I still am young and lack experience;
　　　You both are older and know more than I.
　　　I've much to learn, and how can I be fit
　　　To be allowed to carry on the work
　　　Of our great Master's wisdom? No, dear sir,
　　　I feel my great unworthiness too much
　　　To stir in you a cause for jealousy.
　　　It is enough for me if I can serve him;
　　　That is high honor and great privilege.

Lu.　I have no grudge, Yen Hui, and if I had
　　　I would suppress it, for you are too dear
　　　To mine own heart.

Li.　[*Aside*]　　Why waste this sympathy
　　　On yonder gosling?

Kung.　　　　　And now especially
　　　Since our great Master has been called to office
　　　We must not split but firmly stand together.

Yen.　I am so glad the master did not deign
　　　To serve the state when called on by Yang Ho.
　　　Yang Ho was a usurper. He it was
　　　Who had Duke Chao expelled, and then deprived
　　　Him of his throne, and caused all the confusion

In our state Lû.   He wanted but the name
Of K'ung Fu Tze,—K'ung's fair untarnished name,
To shield and justify his unjust rule.

Exit Lî, whose departure is observed by the others.

Kung.   Who was that?

Lu.   Was't not the Master's son?

Yen.   It was indeed K'ung Lî.

Lu.   He seems to have
No tittle of his father's noble spirit.

Yen.   Oh, he's not bad; he's but indifferent.
He does not know the worth of his great father.
He would have liked the Master to accept
The offer of Yang Ho.   And for a while
K'ung wavered, for he deemed it possible
To change the man, to make him do the right.
He hoped he might convert the unscrupulous
By acting as his mentor and adviser.
Once slyly said Yang Ho to K'ung Fu Tze:
"Can he be called benevolent who leaves
His jewels in his bosom and his country
In worse confusion?"   "No," our Master said.
Yang Ho continued: "And you want employment
But waste your opportunity.·   Our years
Slip quickly and the months pass by—accept!"
The Master then replied: "Your words seem true,
Perhaps I ought to enter into office."

Kung.   The Master wavered; yea, he was inclined
To accept the tempting offer of Yang Ho.
But I prevented it.   I pointed out
The vicious character of Yang and that
The cause of a usurper should not be
Encouraged or supported.   But since then
The righteous heir, Duke Ting, is reinstated.
And happily Duke Ting has found employment
For K'ung Fu Tze in this our state of Lû.

Yen.   When K'ung Fu Tze first served as governor
Of the small district at Chung-Tû of Lû,
What great reform was then at once accomplished!
Things dropped in streets were not picked up or
  stolen;
The strong did not make evil use of power,
The merchants used right weight, the old were
  honored
And womanhood respected.   Above all,
All funeral observances were strictly
And piously observed.

Kung.   Yea, that was good,
But better still was the establishment
Of our young duke's authority.   The barons
Had grown too powerful.   But K'ung Tze broke
Some of their castles where they bade defiance
And humbled them.   Thus spread our Master's
  fame
And now K'ung Tze commands the confidence
Of our good duke, His Royal Highness Ting,
Holding the place of Minister of Justice.
The other princes now begin to fear
That Lû, our little country, will outshine
In glory all the others.   Yea, our neighbor,
The Duke of Ch'i, would gladly conquer Lû.

Yen.   He won't succeed.

Lu.   He may.   We cannot tell.

Yen.   I see no danger, friend.

Kung.   The Duke of Ch'i
Is filled with hate against Duke Ting of Lû.
And do you still remember how our Master
Defeated Ch'i's intrigues at Chia-Ku,
The meeting place of the two sovereigns?
The Duke of Ch'i would have imprisoned Ting,
Had not our Master with his innate wisdom

Defended justice to protect our cause.
Since then Duke Ting has confidence in K'ung.

Kung. The danger is not past, for our Duke Ting
Is like the rest.

Yen. What do you mean, friend Kung?

Kung. Beauty to Ting goes always before duty*
I learn the Duke of Ch'i will send a present
Of thirty spans of steeds—you know the Duke
Loves racing horses; and of eighty damsels.
With song and dance they will so entertain
The Duke as greatly to distract his soul
And make him hate the very name of virtue.

M. I. The Duke has heard of it, but is determined
Not to receive the present. If he did
Our Master could not stay. Here comes K'ung Tze.

They bow low. Enter CONFUCIUS.

C. I greet you, friends, and above all Yen Hui,
Thou most affectionate, best of my students.
At last my time has come: at last I have
An opportunity to prove my doctrine.
His Royal Highness Ting, our noble ruler
The Duke of Lû, lends me his ear and listens
To the advice I give.

Lu. We know it, sir.
The fame of Lû is growing since Duke Ting
Has made thee counselor of state.

C. I see
Great vistas open now and I shall need
Assistance. Dear Tze Lu, the Duke of Wei
Wants an adviser and he needs a man
Of strength; wilt thou be able to keep order?

* A similar saying was used with reference to the Duke of Wei,
who drove with his frivolous queen, the intriguing Nan-tze, in the
first carriage, and made his guest, K'ung Tze, follow behind. At
the sight of this spectacle the people exclaimed (in Legge's trans-
lation): "Lust in front, Virtue behind."

Lu.   I certainly will try to do my best.

C.   Not every man is fit to do the same,
And different tasks require quite different men.
Thou wilt be in thy proper place, Tze Lu,
So go to Wei, and when thou exercisest
Authority, remember that what thou
Dislik'st in thy superiors, do not
Thyself display to those in thy command.

Lu.   My aim shall be to do thee credit, Master.

C.   I wish to know what every one of you
Would do to realize his highest aim
If he were given full authority.
Tze Lu, do thou speak first.

Lu.   My honored Master,
I would induce the people to be strong,
Would make them self-reliant, energetic
And brave to stand up for the right.

C.   And thou,
Tze Kung, what are the methods thou wouldst use?

Kung.   With your permission, I would guide the people,
And I would teach them the right way.

C.   Yen Hui,
Wouldst thou approve the methods of thy friends
And fellow students? Both are men of talent.
Tze Lu is full of courage, and Tze Kung
Persuasive in his manner as a teacher.

Yen.   My Master, I would like to find a sage
Upon the throne, whose counselor I'd be;
And I would help him to diffuse instruction
Among the people on the five relations
And on the lessons they imply. I would
Teach every one within my realm the rules
Of music and propriety, would spread
The love of harmony, that they no longer

Would care to have their cities fortified
By wall and moat, but fuse their heavy spears
And swords into the tools for tilling land.
Their flocks would graze unharmed without protec-
    tion
In open fields.   No war would widow wives
And orphan children, and there'd be no chance
For Lu Tze to display his bravery
Nor for Tze Kung to be an orator.

C.   Yen Hui, I prize thy view as the most lofty.
I see that thou hast sounded all the depths
Of wisdom; thou art fittest to become
The true "Continuator" of my doctrine.
I need disciples, men of different type;
I need men of a literary taste
And diplomats, and men of strength and valor;
I need instructors and philosophers,
They all shall be enlisted in the cause—
Our cherished cause, the cause of all mankind;
But thou, Yen Hui, art nearest to my heart;
And 'tis thy love which comprehendeth all,
All wisdom and all courage and all learning,
All oratory and diplomacy.

    CONFUCIUS *walks toward the door, his disciples
    standing on either side bowing, when* Lî, *his son,
    comes from one side upon the stage and passing
    over in the center reaches the door first.*

C.   Lî, son, my only son, how does it happen
That thou tak'st precedence before thy father?
Hast thou not read the books of Odes wherein

    [Lî *returns, shakes his head and bows with a con-
    trite expression.*]

Thou canst become acquainted with the spirit
Of ancient sages, emperors and nobles?
They were distinguished by propriety
And strictly courteous behavior, son.
They never would have taken precedence

Before their betters, nor before their parents.
Remember, son, and read the books of Odes.

Lî steps aside and allows his father and the disciples to enter. He stays behind.

Lî. [*Shaking his head*]
He is a sage, I doubt not; he's a scholar;
But he is always preaching, moralizing
And talking wisely. I am sick of it.
It bores me, it annoys me. How shall I
Find time to read the book of Odes? I must
Be filial, must behave decorously;
I must observe rules of propriety—
There is no leisure left for anything.

Enter an old man (O. M.) with his son (Son).

O. M. Pray, sir, is here the court where I can find his high honor, the Lord Minister of Justice?

Lî. Do you refer to K'ung Fu Tze?

O. M. Indeed I do.

Lî If so, this is the place. Here K'ung Fu Tze makes his decisions.

Son. Father, let us go hence. If you will only be reasonable, I will do what I can to satisfy you.

O. M. What you can? No, no, I know what that means. You shall do what you must. You are my son, and you must obey. K'ung Fu Tze teaches filial piety and he will punish you severely if he hears my case. You must surrender completely. It is not sufficient to do what you can.

Son. Father, let us go back, I am afraid.

O. M. I will not go back. I will complain of you, and his Honor will deal with you as you deserve. He will probably put you in the stocks; your feet and your hands will be locked and you will carry a placard, "Punished for lack of respect to his father," or something like that. I will send your friends to the marketplace to gaze at you and you will become a public example for the whole town. All your neighbors will gather around you and mock you.

Son. Father, let us go home.

O. M. No, no! I will have judgment. K'ung Fu Tze is a wise judge. He will teach you filial piety. He can punish, you know; he had but to have one criminal executed and crime almost disappeared. But he had to have one man, a real criminal, executed. Maybe he will have you executed, too. Think of it. There are so many different kinds of criminal punishment. I do not know what manner he would select. There are five kinds of capital punishment.

Son. O father, let us go. I am not so bad as you make me out. I have the best intentions. I will do all I can.

O. M. No, no. You must stay and hear judgment.

Li. I will call my father, the judge. [*To the father*] He knows of your case, does he not? You were here before?

O. M. Yes! oh yes! He has heard us, but he did not give judgment. He said we should consider our case and come again. So we have come again and here we are.

Li. I will call His Honor. [*Exit*]

Son. Father, let us go home.

O. M. Oh, no, sir; you must stay and hear your doom. His Honor, the judge, will teach you a lesson. May be he will simply give you a flogging.

Son. Oh, father, what wrong have I done to deserve any punishment at all?

O. M.   Oh, son, son! Do you not know that it is very
wrong to contradict your father and to quarrel with
him? Think of it! That is what you've done.
You have quarreled with your father, with *me*, with
your *own father!*

> *Enter* Confucius, *followed by magistrates and his
> disciples. Seats himself before the screen. The
> old man and his son prostrate themselves.*

C.   You have come back, you two, to hear my judgment,
But I am loathe to give it. I will wait
Till ye among yourselves have peaceably
Arranged your quarrels.

O. M.   But, sir, he is my son,
I am the father of this obstreperous boy.

C.   [*Slowly*]   I see you are!—I understand that you
Have educated this your wayward child.
He may be bad. But, say, who bears the guilt
If not the father who has failed to teach
His son the rules of filial piety?
My judgment is to send you both to jail
And keep you there until you have made peace.

O. M.   What do you say, your Honor? Hear I right?
Do you regard me guilty, me the father,
Of this my son's great faults?

C.   Indeed I do
And I shall punish you e'en as severely
As him.

O. M.   Me? Me, the father?

C.   Yes, indeed,
And, as it seems to me, this is but fair.

O. M.   Let us go home, your Honor: I believe
I can persuade my son to better living.

C.   Go home, and do not dare to come again
Without a good and real cause. The judges

Are not installed to hear paltry complaints.
Where fathers are true fathers and where sons
Are sons, there is no need of courts and judges.

Exeunt old man and his son. Music in the distance.

C.   What do those sounds portend?

Lu.   I'll see, my lord. [*Going to the door and looking out*] There is a festive procession coming, lord. It seems to me the music they have intoned is frivolous.

C.   Indeed the tune is frivolous. Who is this company of female minstrels?

Kung.   My lord, I know. I see it now. These ladies are the singing damsels which the Duke of Ch'i has sent to our Lord Ting, the Duke of Lû. There are the thirty span of horses, too. Oh, how they prance! And here appears Duke Ting himself.

C.   I fear my hour has come, I must withdraw.
The Duke is sick of virtue, sick of me,
Sick of good government. Here is no longer
A place for me. I'd better leave the field
To sport and to frivolities, to vice,
To flatterers and to these singing damsels.

C. retires slowly to a corner of the stage, followed by his disciples. The armed bailiff of the court steps aside. The music continues. Enter DUKE TING *(Ting) with retinue and singing damsels.*

Chorus of damsels:

    Taste the sweets
    Life can give;
    Laugh and love
    While you live;
    Taste the joys
    Which we bring,
    While in glee
    Merrily
    Songs we sing.

Join us in our wanton play! Hi ho!
And enjoy life while you may. Hi ho!

CONFUCIUS *and retinue exeunt.* TZE KUNG *remains on the stage, and approaches the Duke.*

Kung. Duke Ting, most Royal Highness, hear me speak.
I have for you some news of great importance.

Ting. What can be more important than the beauty
That now surrounds us? But speak on, Tze Kung.

Kung. Your councilor, your Highness, K'ung Fu Tze,
Who has done glorious service in your state
Will take his leave unless these damsels go.

Ting. Indeed! Think you that K'ung Fu Tze will go?
I shall be glad to so be rid of him.
He acts as my bad conscience and he grudges
My every joy in life; and me he blames
For every mishap, every accident.
When our ancestral temple burned, he claimed
That my ancestors were enraged at me
And would refuse me further help. They were
No better than I am.
                    And all my neighbors
The Dukes of Ch'i and Wei, the emperor
At Lo and all the princes, enjoy themselves,
Why should not I? And you, my friend, Tze Kung,
You should be wise enough to understand
That drinking vinegar instead of wine
Is not a sign of virtue but of folly.
Come, Kung, and join me in my gaity;
Be my companion in the place of K'ung.

Kung. No, sir; I cannot. I would rather starve
With K'ung the sage than live in opulence
On royal bounties here amid these pleasures.
So fare you well! We leave you to your pastimes.

The damsels again dance.

Chorus of damsels:

> Taste the sweets
> Life can give;
> Laugh and love
> While you live;
> Taste the joys
> Which we bring,
> While in glee,
> Merrily,
> Songs we sing.
> Join us in our wanton play!   Hi ho!
> And enjoy life while you may!   Hi ho!

SCENE II.

A Scene on the Road, in 497.   CONFUCIUS *is seen on his travels.*

Kung. How grand this scenery of Tai San,
The mountain range which separates me from Lû!

C. How beautiful those cliffs, but difficult
They are to travel through, impervious to the foot.
Hand me my lute, friend Kung.

Kung.   Here 'tis, dear Master.

C. [*Plays lute and in a melodramatic voice recites the poem of Tai San*]

> Would rise to the lofty peak;
> Ravines and cliffs debar.
> So truth though ever near
> Is to the seeker far.
> How wearisome to me
> Those tangling mazes are.
> I sigh and look around,
> The summit in full view:
> With woodlands it is crowned
> And sandy patches, too,

And there stretch all around
The highlands of Lian Fu.
Thickets of thorns prevent
Any ascent.
No axe is here
A path to clear;
The higher we are going
The worse the briars are growing.
I chant and cry,
And while I sigh
My tears are freely flowing.

Kung.   My Master, do not yield to gloomy thoughts.
Perhaps the crazy man of Tsu was right,
That you had best the bygone left unmended.

C.   What did he say?

Kung.   He spoke of you in a little verse, in tone humorous,
almost satirical, but there was much truth in his
words.   He sang:

"O Phoenix, oh Phoenix, thy virtue is pinched!
The bygone is ended and cannot be mended:
But truly the future can still be clinched.
Cease, ah! continue not!
For statesmen today are a dangerous lot."

You took a deep interest in him at the time.

C.   I did, indeed, and his queer rhyme is true.
Virtue is pinched and statesmen verily
Are dangerous.

Kung.   And, Master, let me add,
Truly the future can and must be clinched.
You stand up for the right and I believe
The right must finally be recognized.

C.   Tze Kung, see here.   These fragrant orchids
Grow by the wayside mixed with common grass.

Flowers they are of royal worth, but here
They stand unheeded. Such is the sage's fate.

[*He takes his lute and plays. He sings:*]

So gently blow the valley breezes
  With drizzling mist and rain,
And homeward bound a stranger tarries
  With friends in a desert domain.
Blue heaven above! for all his worth
Is there no place for him on earth?

Through all the countries did he roam
Yet found he no enduring home.
  Worldlings are stupid and low,
  They naught of sages know.
So swiftly years and days pass by,
And soon old age is drawing nigh.

Analects, III, xxiv.

ACT V.

SCENE I.

The Garden of Confucius in 479 B. C. A table
with a lute and two chairs. In the background
a house from which CONFUCIUS *is coming. He*
looks feeble and carries a staff. Dragging his
staff, he approaches the table and sits down. His
appearance is worried and he lets his fingers run
over the lute. Enter TZE KUNG.

Kung. My Master, oh, my good, beloved Master,
How did you pass the night?

C.   Tze Kung, my friend,
Why do you come so late?

Kung.   Master, I thought
You needed sleep; but you have risen early.

C. I dreamt ill-boding dreams.

Kung.   You are not well,
And you were restless in your sleep last night.

C. I dreamt that I was sitting in the hall,
Between the central pillars, offerings
Before me, as was custom of the Yin.
According to the ancient ritual
The dead was treated as a guest and placed
Above the eastern stairs, but then the Yin
Regarded him as host and guest at once,
And so they coffined him between the pillars,
Down in the hall. The Chow treat him as guest,

        So now he's placed on top the western stairs.
        I am a man of Yin and I belong,
        Between the pillars in the hall. That dream
        Portends the truth. My time has come to die.

Kung.   Not yet, my Master.

C.   Life has been a failure;
        My son is dead and he accomplished naught.
        But worse was the bereavement which I suffered
        Through the demise of my belov'd Yen Hui.
        He was too gentle for this world of trouble;
        Too kind, too noble and too wise. His hair
        Bleached early, ere he reached his thirty years,
        And when but thirty-one he passed away,
        He who should have succeeded me. 'Tis he
        Who was my best disciple. Since he died
        I feel that heaven has rejected me.

Kung.   My dear old Master, do not speak in gloom.

C.   I speak but as I feel. In better days
        I used to see, when seated at the table
        At dinner time, before me at my place
        The noble countenance of Yao Ti;
        And when I raised my eyes I plainly saw
        The great Shun on the wall. I have not seen
        The Duke of Chow in dream as formerly,
        He was a blessing in my life, a source
        Of comfort, but I am as if abandoned
        By all the spirits of the past, the heroes
        Of our antiquity, our ancient culture.

Kung.   You are discouraged by disease, good Master.
        Remember, you are one of our great men.
        You are a sage, yea truly *the* Great Sage.
        As great as any one among the ancients.

C.   I dare not rank myself among the sages
        Nor with the men of perfect virtue, Kung.
        I simply strive to be a teacher, patient

And diligent. I love the ancients dearly.
And am but a transmitter, not a maker.
The best of me is but a composition
Of greater ones that have preceded me.

Kung.　Your declaration proves your modesty,
For certainly the greatness of the past
Has taken its abode in you.

C.　　　　　　　　　　　　Yea, Kung.
This much is true, that after great Wen Wang
Heaven revealed the truth in me: and heaven
Will not allow the cause of truth to perish.

Kung.　The glory of the past will never die!
Have you not left us treasures everlasting?
You have collected the five sacred scriptures
And also the four books; you have instructed
In your great doctrines many worthy men.

　　Enter K'ung Chî *(Chî), the grandson of Con-*
　　fucius.

Chî.　Do I intrude?

Kung.　　　　　Your grandfather's not well.

C.　K'ung Chî, my grandchild, you are welcome, boy.

Chî.　Grandfather, can you spare me a few moments?

C.　I'm listening, my boy, what is your wish?

Chî.　I want to have instruction in your doctrines.
It is but proper that a child should learn
His father's trade, his business or profession,
Why should I be excluded? Your life's aim
Is so much grander, nobler, so much higher,
Than that of others. All the more I should
Become proficient in the work you do.

C.　You still are young, my boy, but I consent,
For I feel confident that you will take
The place of my deceased disciple Yen,

My much beloved, greatly lamented friend,
Tze Yüan.

Kung.   Take here some of grandfather's books
And read them, boy. You may not care for this,
The book of Rites, nor for the Odes, but here
The book of History will please you surely.

Chî.   Thank you, dear sir. [*Turning to Confucius*]
Thank you, grandfather, thank you very much.
But I should also like to have the Odes. E'en in the
book of Rites I'm interested.

    Goes off with the books.

Kung.   Posterity will yet hear of K'ung Chî,
The grandson of the greatest sage of China,
And thou, dear Master, with such a descendant
As Chî shouldst not complain. Do not expect
That thou canst be successful during life,
For while thou livest, jealousies will be,
There will be puny minds who grudge thee honors
And influence and power. But do not be
Discouraged. Thine ideals are eternal
And they will live when thou hast passed away.
When all the mortal part of thee is gone
Thy truer self will gain due recognition.
Thou wilt be greater after death, dear Master,
Than thou hast been in life, and emperors
Will bow before the grand, divine, deep truth
Which thou hast taught.

    TZE KAO *enters hurriedly and bows to Confucius.*

C.   Tze Kao! So unexpected!

Kung.   We thought you and Tze Lu were still in Wei!

Kao.   Indeed I was, but managed to escape.

Kung.   And where is Lu? Has he remained in Wei?

C.   I fear the worst. Tze Lu is brave and faithful.
I always said that he was not to die

A natural death.   I know the state of Wei
Is in rebellion.   Tell me all you know.

Kao.   The rebels gained, and I advised the Duke
To leave the capital, but he thought little
Of my incompetent advice.   He stayed
And with him Lu.   To tell the story briefly,
The palace was surrounded by a mob
To kill the Duke; and Tze Lu stayed with him.
He charged his enemies with fearless courage,
Felled some, but finally was overcome.
Thereafter fell the Duke himself.

C.   Alas!
Tze Lu! my noble, brave Tze Lu!   But you,
Tze Kao, you escaped the rebels.

Kao.   Perhaps
The mob spared me because I was too ugly;
They did not deem me worthy of their steel.
I am too insignificant and dwarfish.
I am a puny fellow, and against me
E'en criminals are generous and kind
And noble hearted.   Some most envious fellow
Who, having done great wrong, was led before me
While I still served as magistrate in Wei,
And I as judge condemned him by the law
To lose his leg.   Now think!   I on my flight
Was suddenly confronted with that man.
Yea, then I thought I had escaped in vain,
This one-legged scoundrel would surrender me
And make me die a martyr for the cause
Of law and order.   But that he did not do.
He recognized me, greeted me right kindly
And pointed out to me a safe escape.
Said I to him: "And don't you hate me, then,
Because I had you punished?"   "No," said he,
"For you were judge and had to do your duty.
I noticed then," he said, the one-legged villain,
"That you were not ill-willed, as judge in court,

That you were loath to have the law enforced.
You are in trouble now and might be slain,
It would not help me to deliver you
Into the hands of these bloodthirsty rebels.
Flee, then, and save yourself and when you come
To Lû, greet K'ung Fu Tze, your worthy Master.
May the time come when he, the sage, will bring
Peace upon earth and make men well disposed."

C.   Thou art my good disciple, Kao Tze,
         And provest true my doctrines.   I am grateful.

Kao.   The one-legged man deserves your thanks, not I.
         He is a thinker and he argued thus:
         The age is rotten.   That is what he said,
         Rotten, he said.   The princes live for pleasure
         The magistrates and judges are appointed
         For flattery and they take bribes; and truly
         There is no law or order in the world.
         Honesty does not pay, and criminals
         Remain unpunished.   That's the rule, he said.
         "And you, alone," addressing me he said it,
         "And you alone made an exception, sir.
         Wherever such a state of things prevails
         There is no use in striving to be honest,
         And so I went astray.   Yes, I did wrong
         And I deserved the punishment you gave me.
         You told me at the time—and I remember
         The lesson which you taught—let villains know
         That there is law and order in the world,
         That they can make with honesty a living,
         That justice will reward the good and punish
         The evil-doer, then they will reform.
         If I had lived in orderly conditions,
         Nor seen that villains triumph and the good
         Were suffering merely for their meekness' sake,
         I would not have transgressed the middle path."
         That is the reason, venerable Master,
         Why he believed in you.

C.   And, I will add,
You see, my friends, that man is good by nature;
'Tis bad example only that perverts him.
The people would be good if but their princes
Would models prove themselves to be of virtue.

[*Turning to Kao*]

You are of stunted growth, but you are wise;
Your mind is well developed and your wit—
It does me good to see you ere I die.

Kung. We hope to have you with us, and enjoy
Your wisdom still for many years.

C.   No, No,
My course is run. 'Tis but a short time since
A lin was captured by the ducal hunters.
I went to see the noble animal
And truly 'twas a lin. For, as you know,
That noble animal appears whene'er
A sage superior lives upon the earth.
A lin arrived, 'tis said, the very day
When I was born; and now the lin is dead.

Kung. Sir, do not take that fact so seriously.

C.   What other explanation can there be?

[*He takes the lute and plays*]

        Huge mountains wear away, Alas!
        The strongest beams decay, Alas!
        And the sage like grass
        Withers, Alas!

Kung. You make me despondent, Master.   If you lose
        courage
What shall become of me!

[*He sits down, takes the lute and sings.*]

        If the huge mountains crumble, say
        Whither mine eyes shall wend?

If the strong beams will rot away
On what shall I depend?
If sages wither like the grass
From whom shall I then learn, alas?

C. My course is run, and death is near at hand.
I have grown old and feeble. There's no prince
Will offer me the place of his adviser.
My doctrine now is finished.

Kung.   Yea, finished, sir!
It is completed, but it has not ended;
It but begins. The world will come to you,
Sit at your feet and follow your advice.
I see as in a vision the whole nation
Worship the sage of sages. Emperors
Will build you temples and bring offerings.

C. Thou art a comfort to me, Kung, my friend.

[*Kung takes the lute again and sings.*]

Kung. If all would go away
I will not leave my Master;
With him I mean to stay
Through sickness and disaster—
        Aye, aye, forsooth.

Will stay unto the end
Till death the cord has torn,
And as his nearest friend
Will at the tomb still mourn—
        Aye, aye, forsooth.

The rest of all my life shall be
Devoted to his memory—
        Aye, aye, forsooth.

Head of CONFUCIUS *sinks gradually upon the table
as if falling asleep. The background opens and,
surrounded by clouds, the Confucian temple at*

Kü Fu appears with the sage's image. The emperor Kao Tsu, the founder of the Han Dynasty, is seen with retinue. He is offering incense. While the ceremonies are in preparation and the celebrant mandarins are marching up KUNG *addresses* CONFUCIUS.

Kung.   O Master, listen to my prophecy
As in a vision I behold the future!
Thy doctrine will take root in human hearts,
The people flock to thee, and emperors
Will honor thee with holy sacrifice.
A dynasty, a great new dynasty,
Will actualize thy thought, and it will rise
Out of the midst of sturdy commoners.

  [*Turning to the scene that has opened,* Kung *continues.*]

There is a peasant youth; 'tis Liu Pang,
Good-natured, affable and much beloved
Among the villagers of P'ei.   Liu Pang
Is destined to accomplish deeds of greatness.
He leads his men to victory, for great
Prince Hwai, whose cause he has espoused, but heaven
Reserved the throne for the great commoner
Known to the world as Emperor Kao Tî.
I see thee now before me.   Praise to thee
For exercising clemency, for stopping
The fury of the troops, and teaching victors
Stern discipline and mastery of self.
Great Kao, praise to thee, for abrogating
The old barbaric penal code; for being
Humane upon the throne!   Thou comest to teach
The people culture.   Thou hast wisdom learned
From K'ung Fu Tze.   It is the Master's spirit
That moves in thee and guides thy government.
I see thee now approach the sacred spot

Where on the grave of the great saint a temple
Has been erected. Hail Kao Tî! Hail! Hail!

Here follows performance of ritual.

Kung.   [*Turning to C.*]
O K'ung Fu Tze, this is thine after-life.
See here the honor given unto thee,
And listen how an emperor of worth,
The emperor of better generations,
The victor, strong in arms and kind in peace,
The founder of a broad and glorious culture,
Devout and pious, will address thy spirit:

Kao Tî. O K'ung, illustrious and all complete;
Thou ancient Teacher and thou perfect Sage!
Full is thy virtue, absolute thy doctrine.
Among all humankind there's none thine equal.
All kings, rulers and princes do thee honor.
Statutes of justice thou hast handed down.
A pattern art thou unto all of us.
We worship thee in humble reverence,
And filled with awe we sound our drums and bells.